Moody Press

A KING IS RISEN

PATRICIA ST JOHN

Illustrated by Richard Scott

No one had ever ridden the little donkey. He lived at the house by the crossroads, tied up with his mother. If anyone tried to mount him he would kick up his heels and toss him over his head. So it was quite a surprise one day when two men came up the road and started to unloose him.

The master of the house came rushing out. "Hey, what's this?" he shouted. "What do you think you're doing to my donkey?"

"Jesus needs him," said one of the men, and he unhitched the rope.

"Jesus!" said the master. "That's different. If Jesus needs him, you can take him gladly."

The little donkey trotted down toward the town of Jerusalem. "Just let them try riding me," he seemed to say.

But before they reached the town gate, Jesus came out to meet them. "Years ago someone wrote that the real king would ride into Jerusalem on a baby donkey," He said. "Now, before the time comes for Me to die, I want to ride into Jerusalem like that, so that they will all know that I am their true King."

He put His hand on the donkey's neck, and suddenly the little animal didn't want to kick anymore. He wanted to stay with Jesus. He rode quietly into the town carrying Jesus on his back.

But what a noise there was! Jesus had made blind men see and lame men walk, and everybody loved Him. So they all shouted for joy when they saw Him. They broke branches from the trees. They waved them in the air and even threw their coats on the road in front of Him. "Jesus is our Lord," they shouted. "God has sent Him to us." And the children shouted loudest of all.

The little donkey trotted through the noisy crowd, and he never kicked once. Jesus' hand was on his neck, and he wasn't afraid at all.

But not everyone was pleased that the people welcomed Jesus. The teachers and priests were angry and jealous. "Everyone is listening to Jesus," they said. "No one listens to us anymore. And if they make Him king, what about the real king? He won't like it. We can't have two kings."

They called a secret meeting after dark. "Jesus will have to die," they said. "But how can we catch Him? He has done such wonderful things, and the people love Him. We must catch Him secretly at night."

While the secret meeting was going on, Jesus was having supper with His friends. While they were eating, Mary, the hostess, brought a beautiful box of perfume, which she poured on Jesus' head. She wanted to show how much she loved Him. She gave Him the most precious thing that she had.

Jesus was pleased with such love. But Judas, one of His twelve followers, was angry. "What a waste," he muttered. He loved money. He had probably followed Jesus only because he thought that Jesus was going to become king and would make him rich and powerful. But Jesus did not come to make people rich and powerful. He came to make people good and loving. That was why Judas was so disappointed.

Judas knew about the secret meeting. He crept out of the house, along the dark back streets, and knocked at the door of the priest's house. "Let me in," he whispered. "I've come to help you. I know where Jesus sometimes goes at night. How much money will you give me if I tell you?"

"We'll give you thirty pieces of silver," said the priests eagerly.

"Good!" said Judas. "He goes to a garden called Gethsemane up on the hillside. Wait a few nights, and I'll come and take you there."

Jesus also knew about the secret meeting. And He knew that He was going to die. He had just one last night with His twelve disciples. It was a special night, called the feast of the Passover. Jesus said, "We will have a feast too."

"But we haven't got a house," said the disciples.

"We will borrow a room," said Jesus.

When evening came, Jesus and His disciples sat down to have supper. In that hot, dusty country a servant always came in before a feast and washed the feet of the visitors. The disciples looked at each other.

"But we haven't got a servant," they said.

"Well, I'm not going to do it," said one. "I'm not a servant."

"Nor me either," said another.

"Don't look at me," said a third. "Why should I do it?"

No one would do it. They all began to quarrel.

Suddenly Jesus stood up. He tucked up His long robe and poured water into a

basin. "I'll do it," He said. He knelt down in front of each one of them and washed and dried their feet. How sorry and ashamed they all felt!

Then Jesus sat down again and said, "I did that to show you that I want you to love and serve each other, as I did. I want everyone to know that you are My disciples because you love each other so much."

How was Jesus going to tell them that He was soon to die? He did it like this: He took a loaf of bread and broke it. He told the disciples each to take a little bit. "This is like My body that is going to be broken and wounded on the cross," He said.

Then He poured some red wine into a cup and passed it round to them. "This is like My blood that I am going to shed on the cross," He said. "When I am gone, do this often, so that you will never forget that I loved you and died for you."

While they were talking over supper, Judas slipped out. Jesus knew exactly where he had gone. He knew that His enemies would be creeping up toward the garden. He knew that His time had come to die.

"Come," He said to His eleven disciples. "Let's go up to the garden on the hillside."

It was cool in the moonlit garden. The disciples were sleepy. They lay down under the olive trees. But Jesus was not sleepy. He knew that within a few hours He would be suffering a terrible death. He felt dreadfully afraid and alone.

"Peter, James, and John," He said, "please stay awake and pray for Me. Don't leave Me alone."

He went under the trees and knelt down. He prayed to His Father God. "Oh, Father," He cried, "if there is any other way, save Me from hanging on that terrible cross. But if that is the only way, then I will do it."

Three times He prayed this prayer. And then, suddenly, Jesus knew that He was not alone any longer. The angels were all around Him, comforting Him and strengthening Him. He went back to His disciples, but they were all fast asleep.

Jesus woke them. He wanted them to be ready. Already there were lights and the sound of footsteps. Men with torches were hurrying up the hill, waving their swords. Then they stopped. It was impossible to tell in the dark which was Jesus. Only Judas knew. He stepped up to Jesus and kissed Him, pretending to be so friendly. But it was really the sign that His enemies were waiting for.

They were just about to seize him when Jesus stepped forward. "Who are you looking for?" He asked.

"For Jesus of Nazareth," they shouted.

"I am He," said Jesus. And suddenly those wicked men were terribly afraid. They all fell back.

Jesus waited quietly. His enemies got up and came forward slowly and fearfully. But Jesus stretched out His arms to be bound and they led Him away.

When His disciples saw Him taken off, they panicked. They turned and ran away as fast as they could...

... all except Peter and John. John crept along in the dark a little way behind Jesus. Peter followed a long way behind Jesus. He was very, very frightened.

Sitting at supper a few hours before, Jesus had told His disciples that He was going to be killed and that they would all run away. Peter, who loved Him very much, got quite cross about it. "All the others may run away," he had said, "but not me. Never!"

"Listen, Peter," said Jesus gently. "Before the cock crows twice in the morning, you will say three times that you do not know Me."

"Never!" said Peter. "I'd die first."

Peter followed right to the priest's house. Even though it was still dark, the house was full of people and ablaze with light. Outside was a courtyard. The tired servants had lit a fire and were sitting round it.

Peter sat down with the servants and watched the door. What were they doing to Jesus inside? Peter did not notice a girl staring at him. Suddenly she spoke. "You're from Jesus' part of the country," she said. "You must be one of His disciples."

Peter jumped with fright. "I don't know what you are talking about," he muttered. It was just beginning to get light. Nearby a cock crowed.

But the servants were still looking at him. "That's him," said one. "He was with Jesus. I saw him!"

"No, you didn't," cried Peter. "It wasn't me!" He crouched in a corner, and they seemed to forget him. Then another man noticed him.

"Hey, that's one of Jesus' disciples," he said.

Peter was terrified. "I've never even met Him," he shouted. The sun was beginning to rise now, and the cock crowed again.

"It's just as Jesus said," thought poor Peter. Just then the door opened, and Jesus came out. Peter could see that He had been knocked about, but He didn't seem to be thinking about His pain. He was looking straight at Peter. He seemed to be saying, "Don't be too sad. I forgive you."

Peter went out and cried and cried.

Pilate, the Roman Governor, had been waked early, and he was not pleased. The Jews, whom he ruled, were bringing him a special prisoner, and they wanted to kill Him. Only Pilate could give them permission.

Jesus was led in, and Pilate started to question Him. "Are you really a king?" he asked.

"Not in this world now," said Jesus. "I came to teach people the truth."

A messenger came into the room.

"Please, sir, it's a message from your wife," he said.

"Oh, what does she say?"

"She says she has had a dream about this prisoner. She knows that He's good. Don't let the Jews kill Him."

Pilate went to the crowd of Jesus' enemies outside. "I find nothing wrong with this man," he said. "At this time of year you always set one prisoner free. I am going to free Jesus."

"No, no!" shouted the crowd. "Free Barabbas, the murderer! We want Jesus crucified."

"But He hasn't done anything wrong," said Pilate. "Why should He die?"

"He says He's a king," screamed the crowd. "If you set Him free, King Caesar will be angry with you."

Pilate knew Jesus was innocent. But he was also afraid of King Caesar. He gave in. "Take Him away and crucify Him," he said.

So they led Jesus to a hill outside the town. They nailed Him onto a cross and hung Him up to die, while His mother and John and other women who loved Him stood watching and weeping.

But He did not die alone. Two robbers were also nailed onto crosses to die, one on each side of Him.

As the day grew hotter and the long hours passed, one robber began shouting at Jesus. "If You are really God," he yelled, "save Yourself and save us."

But the other man understood. "Don't talk like that," he said. "We are wicked men, and we deserve to die. But this One in the middle has done nothing wrong." Then, turning to Jesus, he said, "Lord, You will very soon be entering heaven. Will You take me with You?"

"Today," said Jesus, "you and I will go into heaven together."

How could Jesus take a wicked man like that into heaven? Well, that was why He came to die. He, who was completely good, was taking the punishment for all the wickedness in the world. He was offering His goodness and forgiveness instead to everyone who would take it.

He stretched out His arms in love to both those murderers. One said, "I don't want You." The other said, "I give You my sins, and I take the love and forgiveness You offer me." And he went joyfully into heaven with Jesus.

A rich man who loved Jesus had a cave in his garden where he himself planned to be buried. "But I would rather use it for Jesus," he said. So the body of Jesus was laid in the cave, and a great stone was placed in front of the entrance.

"And now it's all over," said the sad disciples. "We shall never see Him again."

Two mornings later, some of the women who had seen Jesus die got up very early. Perhaps they were too sad to sleep. "Let's go to His grave," they said. They reached the garden about sunrise, just when the flowers were beginning to open. They had brought sweet smelling spices to put on His body.

"But how shall we get in?" asked one.

The woman in front suddenly stopped. "Wait," she whispered. "The cave is open. Who can have done that?"

"Someone's there," whispered another. They all moved slowly forward, feeling frightened. "The cave is full of light," said a third.

Then they saw two angels in white, sitting in the empty cave.

"Why are you looking for a dead body?" said one of the angels. "Jesus isn't here. He's risen. He's alive! Go and tell the disciples."

All the women turned and ran, except one. Mary Magdalene had been very ill, and Jesus had healed her. She loved Him so much. She couldn't bear to leave until she knew where He was. She could not believe that He was really alive.

Crying bitterly, she turned back into the garden, where the dew was still shining on the flowers. Someone was there, but she couldn't see through her tears who it was. But He spoke to her, and He seemed kind.

"Why are you crying?" asked the man in the garden. "Are you looking for somebody?"

"He's probably the gardener," thought Mary. "Perhaps he can help me." She turned to him. "Someone has stolen the body of Jesus," she sobbed. "Oh, sir, if you know where it is, please tell me, and I will carry it back to the cave."

"Mary," said the man, and suddenly Mary knew. No one ever said her name quite like that except Jesus. She dashed away her tears and knelt in front of Him. "My Master!" she cried joyfully.

"You mustn't stay with Me now," said Jesus. "You must go back to Jerusalem and tell My disciples what has happened." So Mary ran through the bright morning streets. "He's alive! He's risen!" she cried. "I've seen Him!'

But the disciples did not believe her. "Poor thing!" they said. "She's gone crazy with sorrow."

But Peter and John had gone to see, and they knew that the cave was empty. But they still could not believe that Jesus was alive.

"Call the disciples to a secret meeting," they said. And that night, ten of them crept along in the dark to an upper room and locked the door behind them. "Whatever can have happened?" they whispered. "And where is He?"

Then... nobody opened the door, but Jesus was there in the room with them. Or was it His ghost? The disciples were very frightened.

"Don't be afraid," said Jesus holding out His hands. "Look at the marks of the nails. It really is Me." Then fear gave place to great joy as the disciples understood that Jesus was truly alive. "I'm going to send you out into the world as God sent Me," said Jesus. "You are to heal and love and help. And although you won't see Me, I will always be with you."

He stretched out His hands and they knelt in front of Him. They were happier than they had ever been in all their lives. Jesus had come back to them.

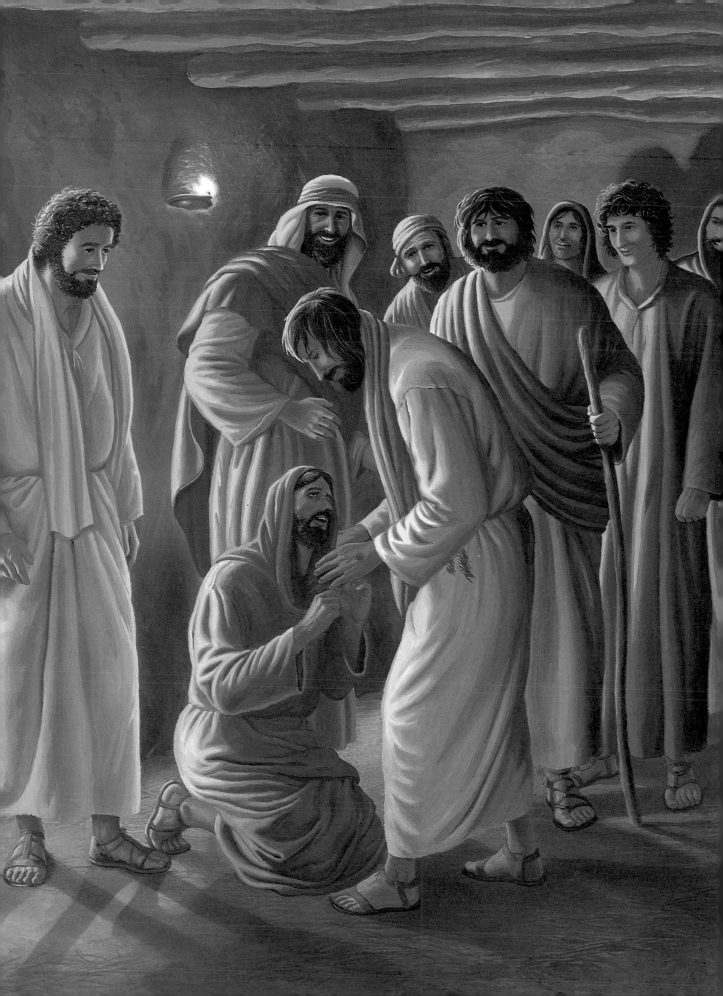

But there were others who loved Jesus, besides the eleven disciples. And they had not yet heard the wonderful news. Cleopas and his friend lived in a little village about seven miles from Jerusalem. That same evening they decided to go home. "There's nothing to stay for," they said sadly. "Jesus is dead."

As they walked they talked. They were rather surprised when a stranger joined them on the road. The stranger said, "What are you talking about? You look so sad."

Cleopas felt rather cross. "Of course we are sad," he said. "Haven't you heard about the terrible things that have happened?"

"What things?" asked the stranger.

"Well, all about Jesus," replied Cleopas. "We thought He was our Savior, but it was all a terrible mistake. The rulers crucified Him three days ago. And that's the end of that."

The stranger looked sad too. "I wonder why you don't believe what the old writers said about the Savior," He said. "They all said that the Savior would have to die before He could save us. Just listen and I'll explain..."

It was all so interesting that they hardly noticed the long walk. Yet when they reached home it was almost dark.

"Good-bye," said the stranger. "I had better be getting on."

Cleopas and his friend looked at each other. It had been such a wonderful walk. "Don't go," they begged. "Come in and have some supper."

They sat down to supper and passed the loaf to the stranger. He stretched out His hand to take a piece of bread, and suddenly they noticed — the nail marks. "It's Jesus!" they gasped, but it was too late. The stranger had disappeared.

"We ought to have known," they cried. "No one else could have talked like that. Quick, we must tell the others."

They ran through the moonlight all the way back to Jerusalem, to where the disciples were meeting. "He's alive!" they cried. "We knew Him when He broke the bread."

Peter had gone back to his fishing. He probably thought that Jesus would never want him to be His disciple again. One night some of the other disciples went with him to help him throw the nets. But it was no good. They worked all night and did not catch a single fish. Tired and disappointed, they started to row back to the shore just before sunrise.

"There's someone standing on the beach," said one of them. "But it's too dark to see who it is."

The Stranger on the shore was calling to them. "Have you caught anything?" He shouted.

"Not a thing," called back the disciples.

"Then throw your nets to the right of the boat, and you'll get plenty." Sure enough, when the disciples threw out the nets, they could hardly pull them back in. They were full of fine, big fish.

But Peter and John were not looking at the fish. They were staring toward the shore. Morning was breaking now, and the sky was all rosy. "It's Jesus," whispered John.

"Jesus?" said Peter. "Then I'm off." He dived into the sea and swam to Jesus.

They all had a wonderful picnic. Jesus had made a bonfire and cooked breakfast for them all. Best of all, He told Peter that He wanted Peter to come back and be His disciple again.

And now the time had nearly come for Jesus to go home to God. But He wanted the disciples to understand that He wasn't really leaving them at all.

"A few days after I go back to heaven, I shall come back to you," said Jesus. "You won't see Me, but My Holy Spirit will come to every heart that loves Me. I will stay with you for ever, filling your hearts with love and courage."

"When I come back to you, I want you to go out and tell everyone that I love them and died for them, and that I am alive now to forgive them and save them. You must start here in Jerusalem and then go farther, till the whole world has heard about Me."

A few days later Jesus led them to the top of a mountain. "Don't forget, I will always be with you," said Jesus, as He stretched out His hands to bless them. Then He rose up into the sky and was hidden by clouds. Jesus had gone home.

The disciples stood looking up until they realized that they were not alone. Two angels stood beside them. "One day Jesus will come back again," they said. "You will see Him coming in the sky, just as he went away." And this is not really the end of the story but the beginning of a new one. The Holy Spirit of Jesus still comes to the heart that loves Him, and Christians are still trying to tell the whole world that Jesus loves them and died for them. And we are still waiting for Him to come back from heaven through the clouds of the sky...

And when that happens, that will be the beginning of yet another story.

You can find the story of the death and resurrection of Jesus in your Bible.

The story of Palm Sunday is in Mark 11: 1–11 and Luke 19: 28–44.
The story of how Judas plots with the priests is in Luke 22: 1–6.
The story of the Last Supper is in Mark 14:12–25 and John 13: 1–38.
The story of the arrest of Jesus in the garden is in Mark 14: 26–52 and John 18: 1–14.
The story of Peter and the servant girl is in Mark 14: 66–72 and Luke 22: 54–62.
The story of how Jesus was brought before the Roman governor, Pilate, is in Matthew 27: 11–31; John 18: 28–40.

The story of how Jesus was crucified is in Matthew 27: 32–56 and John 19: 1–42.
The story of the women who visited Jesus' grave is in Matthew 28:1–10.
The story of how Mary mistook Jesus for the gardener is in John 20: 1–18.
The story of how the risen Jesus met the disciples in a closed room is in John 20: 19–29.
The story of the journey to Emmaus is in Luke 24: 13–35.
The story of the breakfast by the lake is in John 21: 1–19.
The story of how Jesus returned to His Father is in Acts 1: 1–11.

About The Illustrator

Ken Min

Ken grew up on the works of Margret & H.A. Rey, William Joyce, and DC Comics. He was born and raised in Los Angeles and studied illustration at Art Center, College of Design. He has storyboarded for various commercials and animated TV shows such as The PJs, Futurama, and The Fairly OddParents. His illustration work has been recognized numerous times by the Society of Children's Book Writers & Illustrators (SCBWI). In 2012, the first picture book he illustrated, *Hot, Hot Roti For Dada-Ji*, received the Picture Book Honor Award for Literature from the Asian Pacific American Librarians Association (APALA).

These days, you will find Ken illustrating, storyboarding, writing, and dreaming up stories for children.

About The Authors

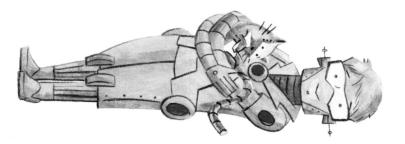

Rana DiOrio

Rana DiOrio has been helping companies grow since graduating from law school. As a lawyer, investor, and investment banker, she has assisted hundreds of management teams in achieving their goals. Becoming a mother inspired Rana to find a way to align her career and values. Her solution was to become an entrepreneur, founding Little Pickle Press in 2009 as a social mission company dedicated to creating media that fosters kindness in children, including her own. Rana sits on the Executive Committee and Board of the Independent Book Publishers Association, and the Advisory Boards of GrapeSeed, Stepping Stories, and Vanderbilt University School of Law. Her personal pursuits include fitness training, practicing yoga, reading non-fiction and children's books, dreaming big dreams and helping other entrepreneurs realize theirs, and, of course, being global, green, present, safe, and kind. She lives in San Francisco, California with The Cowboy and her three Little Pickles. Follow Rana DiOrio on Twitter at @ranadiorio.

Emma D. Dryden

Emma D. Dryden lives in the home in which she grew up in New York City, where she was raised by entrepreneurs. Her father was a self-employed actor and her mother a self-employed writer/researcher. A longtime children's book editor and publisher, Emma spent over twenty years working at a large publishing company before starting her own children's book editorial and publishing consultancy firm, drydenbks LLC, in 2010. Books Emma has edited have won numerous awards, she's an Advisory Board member of the Society of Children's Book Writers & Illustrators, and she speaks extensively on the art and craft of writing for children. Her blog, "Our Stories, Ourselves", explores the connections between the human experience and the writing experience. What Does It Mean To Be An Entrepreneur? is her debut picture book. Visit Emma at www.drydenbks.com.

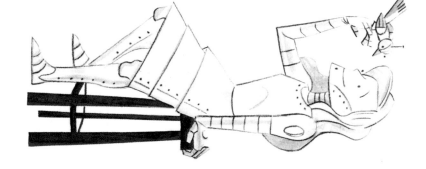

Little Pickle Press

Environmental Benefits Statement

This book is printed on Appleton Utopia U2:XG Extra Green Paper. It is made with 30% PCRF (Post-Consumer Recovered Fiber) and Green Power. It is FSC®-certified, acid-free, and ECF (Elemental Chlorine-Free). All of the electricity required to manufacture the paper used to print this book is matched with RECS (Renewable Energy Credits) from Green-e® certified energy sources, primarily wind.

Little Pickle Press saved the following resources in green paper, cartons, and boards:

trees	energy	greenhouse gases	wastewater	solid waste
Post-consumer recovered fiber displaces wood fiber with savings translated as trees.	PCRF content displaces energy used to process equivalent virgin fiber.	Measured in CO_2 equivalents, PCRF content and Green Power reduce greenhouse gas emissions.	PCRF content eliminates wastewater needed to process equivalent virgin fiber.	PCRF content eliminates solid waste generated by producing an equivalent amount of virgin fiber through the pulp and paper manufacturing process.
44 trees	20 mil BTUs	3,793 lbs	20,567 gal	1,377 lbs

Calculations based on research by Environmental Defense Fund and other members of the Paper Task Force and applies to print quanities of 7,500 books.

Certified

B Corporations are a new type of company that use the power of business to solve social and environmental problems. Little Pickle Press is proud to be a Certified B Corporation.

We print and distribute our materials in an environmentally friendly manner,

using recycled paper, soy inks, and green packaging.

Our Mission

Little Pickle Press is dedicated to creating media that fosters kindness in young people—and doing so in a manner congruent with that mission.

Media For A Better World

And spread the word . . . .
If we support entrepreneurs, our world will be even more diverse, interesting, and creative.

So let's encourage each other to discover
if we have what it takes to be an entrepreneur.

and being brave and
determined enough to create
an innovative solution.

Being an entrepreneur means identifying a need

. . . feeling confident about exercising your own judgment.

. . . working harder than you ever imagined—all while feeling great joy.

... striving for excellence.

. . . staying positive and excited about the possibilities.

. . . having the humility to learn from your mistakes.

. . . taking risks.

. . . loving to learn and being curious.

. . . . moving forward although you are afraid.

. . . saying, "Yes, I can!" when others are saying, "No, you can't."

. . . following your dream
wholeheartedly and unwaveringly . . .

even if it seems impossible.

. . . . thinking differently
and having original ideas.

. . . taking the initiative
to solve a problem.

Being an entrepreneur means . . .

Does it mean
speaking French?
No!

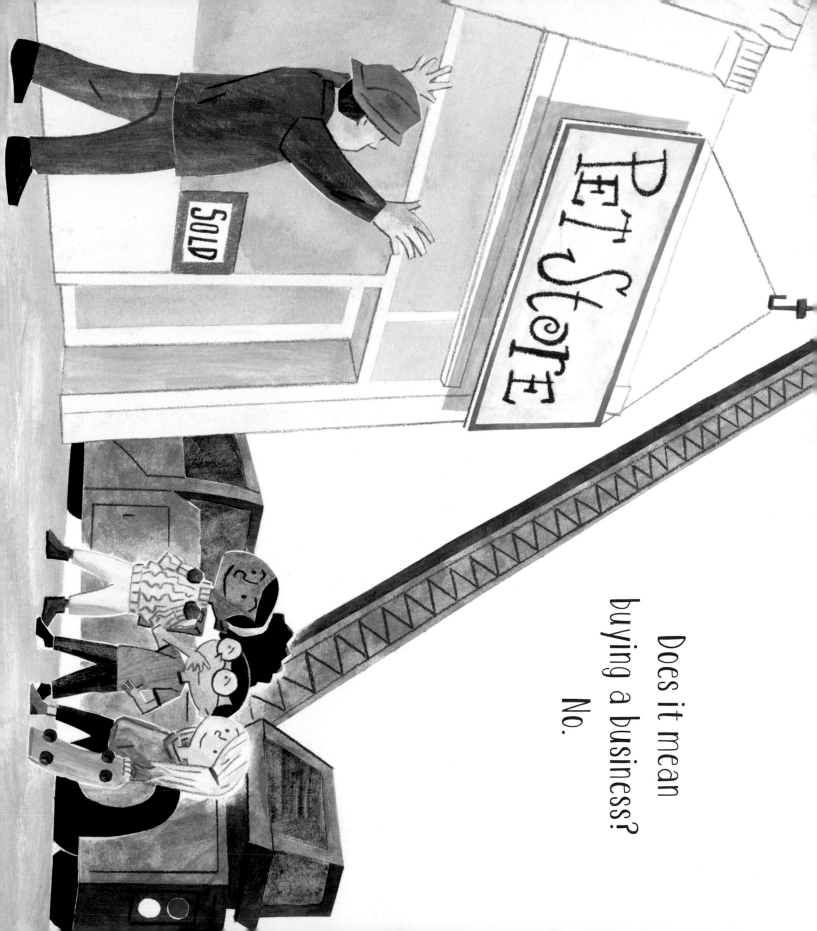

Does it mean
buying a business?
No.

Does it mean making lots of money? No.

What does it mean to be an entrepreneur?

WHAT DOES IT MEAN TO BE AN ENTREPRENEUR?

By Rana DiOrio & Emma D. Dryden

Illustrated by Ken Min

Little Pickle Press

For my Cowboy, who inspires my dreams, believes I can make them come true, and helps me realize them.

– R.D.

In memory of my parents who were entrepreneurial spirits; with thanks to my co-author Rana DiOrio for the collaborative fun; and with love and gratitude always to Anne, my inspiration and forever partner on the journey.

– E.D.D.

For Jillybean.

– K.M.

ISBN 978-1-939775-12-2

13 12 11 10   1 2 3 4 5 6 7 8 9

Printed in the United States of America

Little Pickle Press, Inc.
3701 Sacramento Street #494
San Francisco, CA 94118

Please visit us at www.littlepicklepress.com.

Library of Congress Control Number: 2015042677
Library of Congress Cataloging-in-Publication Data
Names: DiOrio, Rana, author. | Dryden, Emma D., author.
Title: What Does It Mean To Be An Entrepreneur? | by Rana DiOrio and Emma D. Dryden.
Description: San Francisco: Little Pickle Press, 2016 | Series: What Does It Mean To Be . . . ?
Identifiers: LCCN 2015042677 | ISBN 9781939775122
Subjects: LCSH: Entrepreneurship—Juvenile literature. | Businesspeople—Juvenile literature.
Classification: LCC HB615 .D565 2015 | DDC 338/.04—dc23